Yellow Elder

DERRY EVANS

Copyright @2022 by (Derry M. Evans)

All rights reserved. No part of this book may be reproduced in any form or by any electronic or mechanical means, including information storage and retrieval systems, without permission in writing from the publisher, except by reviewers, who may quote brief passages in a review.

This publication contains the opinions and ideas of its author. It is intended to provide helpful and informative material on the subjects addressed in the publication. The author and publisher specifically disclaim all responsibility for any liability, loss or risk, personal or otherwise, which is incurred as a consequence, directly or indirectly, of the use and application of any of the contents of this book.

WORKBOOK PRESS LLC
187 E Warm Springs Rd,
Suite B285, Las Vegas, NV 89119, USA

Website:	https://workbookpress.com/
Hotline:	1-888-818-4856
Email:	admin@workbookpress.com

Ordering Information:
Quantity sales. Special discounts are available on quantity purchases by corporations, associations, and others. For details, contact the publisher at the address above.

Library of Congress Control Number:
ISBN-13:   978-1-957618-46-3 (Paperback Version)
               978-1-957618-47-0 (Digital Version)

REV. DATE: 02/02/2022

YELLOW ELDER

By Derry M. Evans

PREFACE

Upon these pages, you will find,

words and verses to soothe your mind.

Thoughts and phrases rather rare,

especially written for one to compare.

Ponder as you read and savor the strength,

of each written statement despite the length.

Grasp moments of reality as I am sure they will be,

frequent unbelievable and helpful you will see.

Introduction

"To everything there is a season, and a time to every purpose under the heaven:

A time to be born, and a time to die; a time to plant, and a time to pluck up that which is planted;

A time to kill, and a time to heal; a time to break down, and a time to build up;

A time to weep, and a time to laugh; a time to mourn, and a time to dance;

A time to cast away stones, and a time to gather stones together; a time to embrace, and a time to refrain from embracing;

A time to get, and a time to lose; a time to keep, and a time to cast away;

A time to rend, and a time to sew; a time to keep silence, and a time to speak;

A time to love, and a time to hate; a time of war, and a time of peace."

Ecclesiastes 3:1-8 KJV

As the writer of the book of Ecclesiastes says, there are many seasons in our lives. The poems in this book seek to speak to the changes and the seasons that have come our way.

Dedication

This collection of poems is a tribute to my parents; Mr. Samuel H. Evans and Mable Scott Evans, whose guidance still lives on.

Also in memory of my two older siblings; Charles A. Evans and Rosita L. Burrows, whose passing have left vacancies unable to be filled.

Content

Preface

Introduction

Dedication

Section A: Missing Links

    Facing Alzheimer's

Section B: Family Affairs

    Illegitimacy

    Love

    Loneliness

    Family Fellowship

    Messages: 1. Parents to Daughter

                     2. Daughter to Parents

Section C: Focus on the Creator

    My Father's World

    The Promised One

    Human Race

    Creator Vs Man

Section D: A Glimpse of My Homeland

    My Isles of June

    The Bahamas

Section E: Nature

    Ocean Breeze

    Gentle Wind

    Late Fall

    Nature in Action

    Sunset

    At the Sea Shore

    Images of a Storm

Section F: Family Roots

    Mother Mae

    Daddy Sam

Section G: Colleagues

    Transition: Transferring

        Retiring

    In Memory of a Colleague

Section H: Memoirs of Daddy

    John Shannon

    My Sailor

Section A: Missing Links

Facing Alzheimer's

The absence of recognition stared blankly towards me
From eyes that once gleamed with pleasure whenever we met.
The movement of eyeballs showed nothing except the motion.
A faint smile twitched briefly across thin weather-beaten lips,
That once would have been a hearty laugh.

The bony fingers clutching mine
showed signs of wear and tear.
The grip was strong and brought to mind, an infant clinging to its mom
in fear.
No sound is heard as she speaks no more,
But lays and stares in oblivion's trance.
Daily, weekly, monthly, and now it's been years,
Watching her waste away slowly from reality.

It's painful, confusing, and rough seeing her in this state,
But God knows best the reasons why
Such problems affect the human race.
He also knows best how much we can take,
And one day, we will have the answers
to all the questions, we are afraid to ask,
when from this earth we all have passed.

Received 'Literature of Achievement Award' – Voices of Many Lands, N.Y. 1995

Section B: Family Affairs

Illegitimacy

Like bundles of cotton
As sweet as a rose,
As soft as the morning dew;
A mother cuddles a baby new.
With tears in her eyes, she holds him close
and thinks of their future which she fears most.
The father had left on hearing the news,
of responsibility for which he cared less.
He'd rather quit and be free as a lark,
than stay and into wed-lock embark.

Like scars of a wound,
As firm as immovable,
As continuous as forever;
The traits of illegitimacy remain.
With twangs in her heart, she reclines,
and shuts out the future which she fears most.
The father leaves for greener pasture,
and settles his conscience regardless of the matter,
He'd rather quit and be free as a lark,
than stay and into wed-lock embark.

Love

Love is like a sword

piercing through a satin pillow,

it kindles like fire coal;

when it meets a blade of willow.

It engulfs a mind and takes control,

Love penetrates, inflames, and surrounds;

And sometimes ends like petals on the ground.

Love is like a rose,

It doesn't just appear,

Give it time to grow

Or it ends in tears.

Loneliness

Once an infrequent visitor,

Now a permanent resident,

has taken up the space that once was filled with laughter.

Standing out like a single shoal

That welcomes the flow of ebbing tide,

Echoing like the ruins of an abandoned house

Where no one sings or laughs within,

Reminding one of an old homestead,

Where the lone rocking chair moves slower,

As its only occupant drifts off into a wavering stupor

Tugging at your heart on a cold winter's night

Or on top of a hill watching an eagle's flight,

Wherever you are the shadows evolve;

and engulfs the existence of one's control.

Family Fellowship

Some of the most precious moments of my life
are the gathering of my family on a warm Summer's night.
Through the years, we have talked, laughed, and cried,
And did other things we thought we should.

Experiences we shared and problems we solved,
are specific reasons why we have survived.
The support and concern we shared so willingly,
will sustain us for the rest of our lives.

Unconditional love grew all through the years,
which blossomed from out each family affair.
And locked in each breast are memories so dear,
Which reminds us of each fellowship rare.

Messages

1: To Parents from Daughter

There comes a time in each girl's life,

when she must try her wings.

She has got to see if she can fly,

Without those "Apron Strings".

I know that time is finally here,

I am happy, yet I am sad.

It seems like only yesterday,

I was your little girl.

2: To Daughter from Parents

Always keep your standards high,

And to yourself be true.

May your every wish and dream,

make life worthwhile for you.

Section C: Focus on the Creator

My Father's World

This is my Father's world,
A beauty to behold,
As nature does her role;
this is my Father's world.

This is my Father's world,
With mountains high and wide,
With lovely flowers on either side;
this is my Father's world.

This is my Father's world,
Its charms are sure amazing,
With cattle on their ranches grazing;
this is my Father's world.

This is my Father's world,
A great celestial globe,
Where astronauts have probed;
this is my Father's world.

The Promised One

Promised of old was the Holy One

He was to be a mighty king,

to change wrong to right was He to come;

that all of Israel again may sing.

The prophet foretold the angel proclaimed

Of the coming forth of the Promised One,

to save the world from sin and shame;

by humanity accepting freely God's Son.

They heard of His coming but knew not the hour

nor yet the place where He would appear,

but they spread the glad news afar;

that all of the world could hear.

Human Race

A man can be distinguished

from his colour as a particular race,

but you cannot see his character in his face;

His mind is hidden until vanquished.

His language plays an important part

but sometimes his features concede,

Then from there, you can proceed

and fit each in his country apart.

Creator Vs Man

Fluffy, white, compact, bulky, and spacious

The clouds from my vantage point,

exhibited various characteristics.

They spanned the sky with grace and obvious flair

and an indication that there's a God out there.

The airplane though large and completely full,

responded to the gravitational pull.

Man versus the creator was evident throughout,

as God demonstrated He alone has total control.

He formed the clouds and created man,

So it is not difficult to understand;

God is in control and not man.

Section D: My Isles of June

My Isles of June

Nestled between Cuba, the Atlantic Ocean, and the Americas,

is where you would find my isles of June;

this tropical archipelago where I love to roam.

The natives exude pride from progress made

by completing foundations their forefathers laid.

Each isle surrounded by turquoise seas,

gives the illusion of jewels on a royal crown;

breezy trade winds fan hot summer days,

while cool, dewy mist soften winter nights

are trademarks that are widely known,

about my "Home"; my Isles of June.

The Bahamas

The Bahamas is an archipelago,
where pineapples in abundance grow;
the seas are warm, the beaches white,
the sunshine is forever bright.

The islands are unspoiled and charming,
Where people produce crops by farming;
And raise their children with pride and joy
While seeing to it that freedom does not alloy.

Our people are courteous and friendly,
thereby making visitors' stay lengthy;
the native dishes are undeniably nice,
especially the tasty peas and rice.

Casaurina trees idealize virgin beaches,
Polished white sand the water bleaches;
Surfers and divers neither fear
When into the turquoise waters they dare.

Amidst the ornaments of Mother Nature,
There are places where tourists venture;
To listen to Goombay Music with Goat-skinned drum
while taking a sip of the native rum.

The accomplishment of Merit Award for outstanding literary achievement from Creative Arts & Science Enterprises, N. Y. 1994

Section E: Nature

Ocean Breeze

How soft is the ocean breeze,

that caresses you gently on the cheek?

No roughness as among the trees;

but softly as a word called meek.

Its scent is sure refreshing,

its taste is surely charming,

with lovely waters far below;

it sets one's little heart aglow.

The ocean breeze is fresh indeed,

It provides a part of each one's need,

And when I look across the seas,

I can't help but love the ocean breeze.

Gentle Wind

A touch indigenous of a dew-laced petal,

crossed my cheek and left a warm tingle

behind on its flight of butterfly wings.

Unaware of the effect, with feathery feet,

it moves along to another victim

and lands as gentle as a baby's breath.

No visible prints, yet I experienced the aura,

of being engulfed, entranced, and pampered

by the satin-soft pat of the gentle wind.

Late Fall

The hues of late September leaves appear

mingled with the myriad of colours of uniforms,

herald the beginning of a new school year;

mothers, teachers, all must be in full gear

as individually they report to duties to perform.

The chill of winds and aroma of coffee pots,

mixed with moans and groans from tiny tots,

tell us that Winter has set in its fangs

while children scamper as the school bell rang.

Nature in Action

I took a walk across an open field
where daffodils, tulips, and wildflowers grew,
while they to rules of nature yield,
all clustered and damp with morning dew.

I took some steps and looked around
upon pine trees, with leaves lustrous and green,
like a precious robe and royal crown
adorning a stately queen.

Looking farther still where mountains stood
with white-capped tops and grassy slopes,
disturbed only by nature and climbers' ropes
from a nearby neighbourhood.

Beneath the mountains in groups of twos,
grazed cattle of various sizes,
and another day dawns brand new
as over the country, the sun rises.

Sun Set

I sat and watched the sun go down

beyond a lonely hill,

the little lambs flit round and round

the swiftly running rill.

I sat and watched the sun go down

behind a lovely hill,

with yellow, melon, turquoise bright

it gave the sky a radiant light.

I sat and watched the sun go down

over a lonely town,

the stillness of the night had grown

over my home town.

At the Sea Shore

The sailboats neatly tied up at their mooring,

Look beautiful on a bright, sunny morning;

sitting on the seashore watching the day dawning,

a sailor sees the captain in command yawning,

Early fishermen selecting their fishing utensils,

while captains trace out their charts with pencils;

the water is calm and clear as crystal,

the scene in one word is delightful.

Images of a Storm

Cloudy skies like a pastel painting,

painted by an amateur painter,

who got his grey and blue mixed up;

and accidentally spilled on spots of black.

Strong winds like an angry woman

lashing out at every tree in its path.

They toss and turn, bending, breaking, snapping,

while debris scatters in various directions.

Huge waves rising, releasing, exploding

and crashing, unleashing onto the shore,

devouring any object that ventures thereon,

and buries it deep in a watery pit.

Section F: Family Roots

Mother Mae

Her smile was warm and inviting

to most persons who stood at her door,

she would invite them to enter

and made them welcome for sure.

She would inquire about their welfare

as she would urge them to tell,

and it would make her happy,

to know that all was well.

There was another side to this lady

She was a strong disciplinarian,

the rules were followed as given;

for one knew the rod was not hidden.

Daddy Sam

He stood tall above the six feet mark

and wore that height quite well.

His were of dual heritage

From his appearance, you could tell.

The dad I knew followed the rules

And made sure his children did too.

His voice was gentle when one obeyed

but was silenced when rules were broken.

That voice was music to our ears

But the silence sent us scampering.

For the calm always came before the storm

which up to this day has made us strong.

Section G: Colleagues

Transition

To Colleagues - Transferring - Retiring

We tread the parts our lives must take
and follow where they lead,
on level roads or rocky slopes
or on a mountain top.

Enroute one's steps would stop and rest
and solid foundations build,
firm, strong, and well-grounded
to endure the test of time.

The curves and holes we often meet
cause pain and discomfort anew,
in the foundations, we have bonded tight
as transitions make one's life incomplete.

In Memory of a Colleague

With gentleness she molded lives,
A task she did with pride.
Her counsel to the many minds,
who sought her help aside.

With creative hands, she did her part,
Without a murmur nor a sigh.
She did it willingly from the heart,
a trait we all admired.

A friend, true confidante indeed,
to many fortunate ones.
The fond memories that now we hold,
the hands of time cannot erase.

Rough though it seems, life must go on,
with all the ups and downs.
But with strength from above, we can go on,
holding thoughts of a friend we all have known.

Section H: Memoirs of Daddy

John Shannon

John Shannon was a sailor
who loved to sail the seas,
he'd stand on deck and sniff the air
enjoying the freedom of the ocean.

When on the land and all at ease
John Shannon was a sportsman.
He'd race his car and take his gal
to any local performance.

One night amid a storm-tossed sea
John Shannon stood on deck,
and prayed for land and love
all of which he could not see.

The ship was tossed and battered
And soon began to sink,
John Shannon's life was fleeting fast
as the angry waters raged.

Nonetheless, he kept the faith
And prayed for all forgiveness,
and lastly one earnest request'
That his naïve life is spared.

About twenty yards beyond the ship
he saw an object floating,
within his direction, the wind was blowing
and with it came the object.

John Shannon's prayers were answered.
He on the raft found refuge,
a passing ship picked him up
and carried him to a safe landing.

My Sailor

He spoke softly between weather-beaten lips.
Sounds barely audible than the ripple of the water
Reached my keen ear and bounced off the bow
Of the sun-drenched boat.
I missed you terribly he said
When the seas seemed endless when the nights
brought misery from the chills.
I would often close my eyes and imagine I was
wrapped up snugly in our cabin on the hill.
I would see your face warmed by the heat
from the fire on the hearth,
as you gently fill our mugs with hot sweet brew,
and all would be well till the sun rose up
and warmed me too.

He focused his attention on the sail,
which gave me a chance to trace my thoughts,
for I too had pangs for his absent role.
No one to check the leak where the roof was really worn,
Or to share the meal that was barely touched
for his nearest meant so much.
I would walk the ridge and talk to the dog
until the sun would set.
The stillness of the night was the utmost fear,
I would toss and turn and count the crickets' call,
As they too tried to conceal their thoughts
of missing mates on this windswept ridge.

His whistling interrupted my thoughts and brought
me to the scenes before me.
The sail looked regal as the boat sailed
briskly on its course.
Mounting each wave and mastering its height with ease.
The craft was guided by a skill that was
Mastered from year to year
The sailor knew the craft and the see as well
as he knew himself
He had built the boat from native wood
grown in his parents' backyard.
He smiled and rubbed his furrowed brow before he resumed his
dialogue.

About the Author

Miss. Derry M. Evans is a former educator. She taught at the elementary level for forty-two years. She studied at the University of Miami and the College of The Bahamas, now renamed the University of The Bahamas.

She is a published author whose story "Brave Sally" is published in the book KIDS READ Short Stories by Horizon Publishing, Toronto, Canada.

Miss Evans is also a contributing author in several anthologies of poetry in the United States. She is the winner of a Merit Award for Outstanding Literary Achievement for the poem, "The Bahamas" published by Creative Arts and Sciences, October 1994.

Her other credits include being the winner of a Literature of Achievement Award for the poem, "Facing Alzheimer's" in the book, Voices of Many Lands, published in 1995.

Derry's hobbies other than writing are traveling, gardening, and sports. She is presently completing the first of two novels.

Yellow Elder

www.ingramcontent.com/pod-product-compliance
Lightning Source LLC
LaVergne TN
LVHW020449080526
838202LV00055B/5394